Isaac Asimov's

21st Century

Library of the
Universe

Fact and Fantasy

BY ISAAC ASIMOV
WITH REVISIONS AND UPDATING BY RICHARD HANTULA

Gareth Stevens Publishing
A WORLD ALMANAC EDUCATION GROUP COMPANY

Please visit our web site at: www.garethstevens.com
For a free color catalog describing Gareth Stevens Publishing's list of high-quality books
and multimedia programs, call 1-800-542-2595 (USA) or 1-800-387-3178 (Canada).
Gareth Stevens Publishing's fax: (414) 332-3567.

Library of Congress Cataloging-in-Publication Data

Asimov, Isaac.
    UFOs / by Isaac Asimov; with revisions and updating by Richard Hantula.
       p. cm. — (Isaac Asimov's 21st century library of the universe. Fact and fantasy)
    Includes bibliographical references and index.
    ISBN 0-8368-3954-4 (lib. bdg.)
    1. Unidentified flying objects—Juvenile literature. I. Hantula, Richard. II. Title.
  TL789.2.A83   2004
  001.942—dc22
                                          2004048238

This edition first published in 2005 by
Gareth Stevens Publishing
A World Almanac Education Group Company
330 West Olive Street, Suite 100
Milwaukee, WI 53212 USA

Revised and updated edition © 2005 by Gareth Stevens, Inc. Original edition published in 1988
by Gareth Stevens, Inc. under the title *Unidentified Flying Objects*. Second edition published
in 1995 by Gareth Stevens, Inc. under the title *UFOs: True Mysteries or Hoaxes?*. Text © 2005
by Nightfall, Inc. End matter and revisions © 2005 by Gareth Stevens, Inc.

Series editor: Betsy Rasmussen
Cover design and layout adaptation: Melissa Valuch
Picture research: Kathy Keller
Additional picture research: Diane Laska-Swanke
Artwork commissioning: Kathy Keller and Laurie Shock
Production director: Jessica Morris
Production assistant: Nicole Esko

The editors at Gareth Stevens Publishing have selected science author Richard Hantula to bring
this classic series of young people's information books up to date. Richard Hantula has written
and edited books and articles on science and technology for more than two decades. He was
the senior U.S. editor for the *Macmillan Encyclopedia of Science*.

In addition to Hantula's contribution to this most recent edition, the editors would like to
acknowledge the participation of two noted science authors, Greg Walz-Chojnacki and
Francis Reddy, as contributors to earlier editions of this work.

Printed in the United States of America

1 2 3 4 5 6 7 8 9 09 08 07 06 05 04

Contents

• UFOs •

We live in an enormously large place – the Universe. It's only natural that we would want to understand this place, so scientists and engineers have developed instruments and spacecraft that have told us far more about the Universe than we could possibly imagine.

We have seen planets up close, and spacecraft have even landed on some. We have learned about quasars and pulsars, supernovas and colliding galaxies, and black holes and dark matter. We have gathered amazing data about how the Universe may have come into being and how it may end. Nothing could be more astonishing.

But that doesn't mean we have solved everything about the Universe. Astronomers puzzle over things they observe with their telescopes and other instruments millions of light-years away. Puzzling events also occur very close to home. Some people have seen strange lights or objects in the sky. These sightings are called unidentified flying objects, or UFOs. What can they possibly be?

What does the object in the sky in this picture, taken in Hawaii, look like to you?

4

UFOs – Fact or Fancy?

Sometimes people see strange objects in the sky they can't explain. Because there doesn't seem to be a ready explanation for the objects, they are referred to as UFOs, or unidentified flying objects.

The present-day UFO excitement started in June 1947, when airplane pilot Kenneth Arnold saw a formation of bright objects skimming mountaintops in the state of Washington. He described them as moving like saucers skipping across water. The name *flying saucers* caught on. But there were other UFO sightings prior to this. Some go very far back in time, and not all of them were reported to look like saucers.

Above: Pilot Kenneth Arnold saw UFOs from his plane one day in 1947.

5

UFOs in History

Hundreds, even thousands, of years ago, what did people think when they looked at the sky and saw things they could not explain? We do not know.

However, vague stories and legends about UFOs have been told for centuries. In the 1500s, people reported seeing spheres and disks in the sky over Germany and Switzerland. The Bible says a fiery chariot appeared as the prophet Elijah was carried up to heaven by a whirlwind. The prophet Ezekiel said he saw four creatures, with strange wheels, come from a fiery cloud.

Above: An artist's interpretation of Ezekiel's vision as a UFO sighting.

Ezekiel's vision – UFOs in the Bible?

In the Bible, in the first chapter of the Book of Ezekiel, the prophet Ezekiel tells of a vision he had. He says he saw four humanlike creatures. Each of them had four faces and four wings. Their legs were straight, but their feet had hooves. What's more, the creatures were accompanied by wheels within wheels that moved with them. As the objects moved, there was a great noise. What did Ezekiel see? Should we conclude that the Book of Ezekiel reports a UFO sighting?

Above: According to reports, on August 7, 1566, a group of round objects appeared in the sky over Basel, Switzerland, and raced toward the Sun. Before vanishing, some of the objects turned toward each other, as if in combat.

Above: Strange disks and spheres reportedly followed U.S. aircraft on bombing missions over Europe during World War II. Sightings were reported on several occasions, and their origin remains a mystery to this day.

UFOs Throughout the World

In 1896, people began reporting that they had seen cigar-shaped objects in the sky that looked like airships. A rash of such reports came from England and New Zealand between 1909 and 1913. Soon, similar reports poured in from many other countries.

Left and below: Aerial photos taken near Nazca, Peru, reveal lines that may look like runways for vehicles from other worlds. Also visible in the area are figures that seem to represent animals and plants (*left*). Many scientists believe that the patterns were actually built long ago — perhaps as many as 2,000 years ago — by people living in the area for use in special ceremonies.

The Great Pyramid — built by aliens?

In about 2500 B.C., the ancient Egyptians built the Great Pyramid. They used about 2,300,000 blocks of stone, each weighing thousands of pounds. No one knows exactly how the Egyptians could have made such a mighty structure with their simple tools. Some people think that aliens from UFOs built the pyramid. But others wonder why such aliens would not have built the structure out of a more advanced material than stone.

Present-Day UFOs

People have been seeing brightly lit objects in the skies for ages. It is not difficult to imagine that UFOs may be advanced vehicles of some sort from worlds far away.

Some people have reported feeling heat, static electricity, sickness, or other odd sensations while they were in the area where the UFOs were sighted.

So what is true and what is imaginary? Unfortunately, it is sometimes hard to know what is really the truth from the various stories that people relate.

Above: A UFO reportedly photographed near Albuquerque, New Mexico, in 1963.

In the mid-1980s, several police officers saw an unusual object in the sky near Belleville, Wisconsin. Radar tracked the object, but no one was able to explain what it was. This photo was taken in Belleville. The UFO has been added by an artist to give you an idea of what the people may have seen.

Above: Cradle Hill, in Warminster, Wiltshire, England, is the scene of several UFO sightings. Cradle Hill was known as a UFO "hot spot" in the 1960s.

Truth or Fiction?

There have been thousands of reports of UFO sightings, but nothing in the way of solid evidence. You would think that with all those ships flying through the air, at least one would have crashed or dropped some evidence to the ground! There have been photographs taken of UFOs, but they are not very clear or reliable.

Then, too, whenever a very sensational sighting is reported, there are suddenly dozens of other similar reports. Some UFO groups argue that these additional sightings confirm the first. They say a UFO announcement may encourage people to come forward with sightings they had been afraid to report earlier. But people often copycat, or imitate, each other and make false statements.

And none of these stories, so far, has produced any real evidence that says, "This came from a UFO!"

Identified Flying Objects

There is no doubt that people sometimes see objects in the sky they don't understand. Many things – such as odd-shaped clouds, ball lightning, comets, the planet Venus, the trails of meteors, burning marsh gases, airplanes, or the lights of distant cars – can seem mysterious, especially when they appear in the dead of night.

In addition, there may be lights in the sky for reasons that scientists do not yet understand or know how to explain.

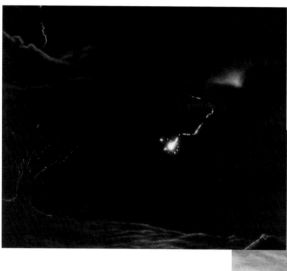

Left and below: Ball lightning and weather balloons are unfamiliar sights to most people.

Control tower to Venus: "You're cleared to land!"

UFO investigator Allan Hendry told this story on an episode of the Public Broadcasting System's show *NOVA* entitled "The Case of the UFOs." Air traffic controllers in a busy airport were expecting the arrival of a flight in the eastern sky during dawn hours. When they spotted the planet Venus out of the control tower window, they radioed it clearance to land! Hendry says this goes to show that "even the best-trained observers can be fooled by this unusually bright planet."

Above: On their way to becoming the first humans to land on the Moon, the *Apollo 11* astronauts spotted this strange object (*at right*) on July 16, 1969. Officials from the U.S. government identified it as a piece of space "junk" from *Apollo*'s Saturn rocket. Others weren't so sure.

Above: High-altitude, lens-shaped clouds can play tricks on the eyes. They may look like something they are not.

Would you be fooled by this fake UFO photo? Not if you saw the whole picture! To create this fake UFO, two paper-plate bowls were stapled together, highlights were added to the object with a felt-tip marker, and a "partner in crime" with the photographer threw the flying saucer.

Right: This man is a UFO hoaxer. His flying saucer (opposite) is a fake.

Is It a Bird? Is It a Plane? No, It's a Fake.

Unfortunately, some people like to get their names in the papers or have fun fooling people. It is easy to take a photograph of a spaceship model so it looks like it is floating in the sky. People can also create fake rows of lights. Sometimes, people make fake UFO pictures by just keeping the camera out of focus, or putting a drop of developer on a negative, or altering an image file on a computer. Some hoaxers are quite skilled at making fake photographs of supposed UFOs.

Many hoaxes have been checked out and dismissed. The more hoaxes there are, the harder it is to believe *any* UFO reports.

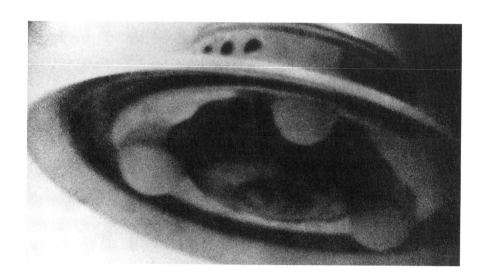

Invasion from Mars!

In 1938, actor/director Orson Welles broadcast a radio drama based on H. G. Wells's science-fiction novel *The War of the Worlds*. "News bulletins" in the show stated that Martian ships were attacking New Jersey and spreading over the United States. In the introduction to the radio play, Orson Welles clearly said, "This is not truth. It is fiction." In addition, no astronomers at the time thought there was advanced life on Mars. But many of the show's listeners believed the story. Large numbers of people in New Jersey got into their cars and fled in panic.

Above: One of the most famous "saucer" shots available was taken by Paul Trent in Oregon on the evening of May 11, 1950. The picture shows an object sailing over a toolshed in Trent's backyard. "It was very bright . . . and there was no noise or smoke," Mr. Trent said of the saucer. Added Mrs. Trent, "It was shiny but not as bright as a hubcap . . . and awfully pretty."

Below: An enlarged view of the object in Mr. Trent's photograph.

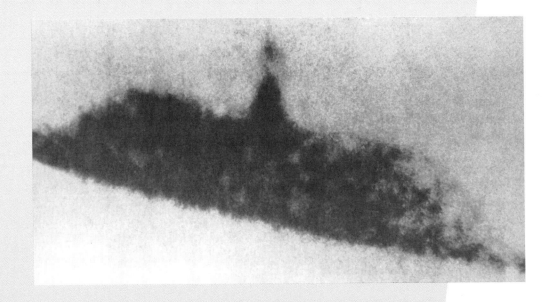

Earth Visitors

Perhaps the most popular definition of UFOs is that they are alien ships carrying beings from other worlds.

We understand enough about our Solar System today to know that if there are beings in outer space, they probably live not in our Solar System but on planets many light-years away. The trip from their world to our world would be extremely difficult, requiring incredible amounts of energy, dedication, and sacrifice.

It is likely that our advanced instruments would detect an actual expedition approaching Earth from great distances. If the many different shapes and sizes of UFOs seen in the past several decades were actually ships from other worlds buzzing our planet, some of them would probably have been identified by now.

Above: A strange object showed up in the sky in this photograph taken at New Mexico's Museum of the Horse in 1996.

What Do You Believe?

Many people think that the government should investigate reports of UFO sightings with great care. After all, there is a possibility that UFOs just might be advanced aircraft developed by some other nation for unfriendly purposes.

Government investigations almost always conclude that there is no proof of actual UFOs. The conclusions usually state that some sightings have natural explanations, some are hoaxes, and some are the result of panic or fear. Many people accept these conclusions. Others, such as astronomer J. Allen Hynek, say that government investigations are not as thorough or honest as they might be. (Hynek, who died in 1986, once investigated UFO reports for the U.S. government.) And still others — mainly people who believe UFOs are alien spaceships — simply refuse to accept such conclusions from the government. They think the government is lying and hiding evidence.

Still, there have been thousands of reports of UFO sightings. Are all of them wrong? Currently, scientists feel there is no real proof that flying saucers from other worlds exist.

Above: UFO researcher J. Allen Hynek felt the U.S. government was not doing enough to investigate UFO sightings.

Below: This mysterious design was photographed in a field at Golden Ball Hill, near Alton Barnes in Wiltshire, England, in 2001. Could it have been made by extraterrestrials? Many such "crop circles" have been found to be hoaxes.

Above: In July 1947, a rancher in New Mexico heard a crash late one night during a storm. The next morning, he found his land littered with debris. Many people thought the debris was from a flying saucer! This painting shows what the rancher may have imagined to be happening outside his window that stormy night.

When is a UFO not an unidentified flying object?

There are many sensational books about UFOs. One, *The Roswell Incident*, tells of an alleged flying saucer crash just a couple of weeks after pilot Kenneth Arnold made his sighting in 1947. A New Mexico rancher found debris that seemed to have come from a crashed saucer. But a closer look at the debris indicated it probably came from a crashed balloon that, according to a later U.S. Air Force investigation, was most likely part of a once top-secret project for monitoring Soviet nuclear tests.

A Continuing Controversy

Many people believe that UFOs are alien spaceships. The excitement surrounding UFO sightings is sensational, and some people like hearing about sensational things.

For example, in 1835, the *New York Sun* reported that a new and powerful telescope had discovered living creatures on the Moon. In fact, the report was a clever hoax by reporter Richard A. Locke. Most scientists already believed the Moon had little or no air or water and could not support life. But thousands of people believed the hoax.

It seems that sensational UFO reports will continue through the ages, and so will the controversy!

Right: These lights in the sky over South Island, New Zealand, remain unexplained.

The end of the world!

In the early 1800s, an American preacher named William Miller studied the Bible and concluded that the world would come to an end in March 1844. Thousands of people sold all their things and waited on a hilltop to be taken to heaven. Nothing happened. Miller predicted a new date of October 1844. Again, nothing happened.

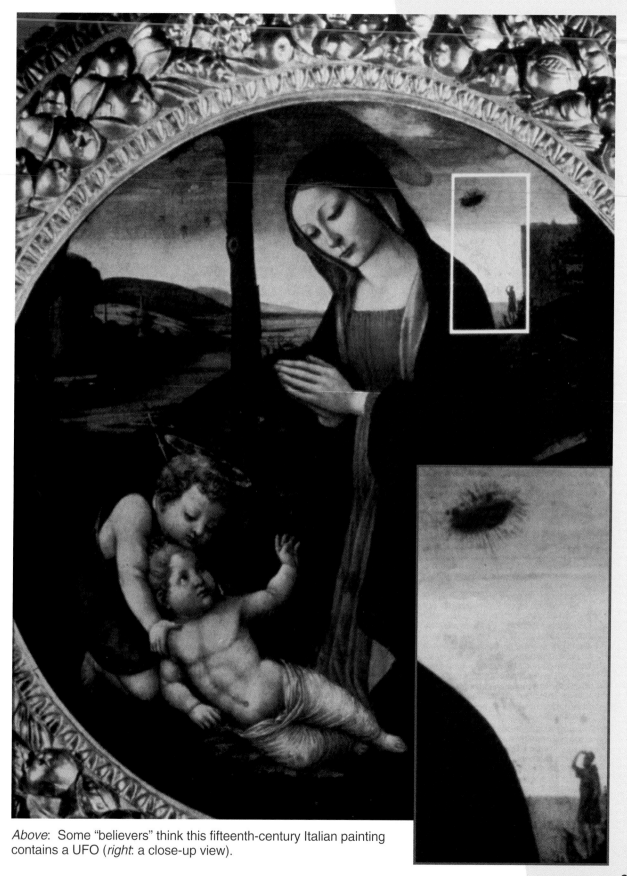

Above: Some "believers" think this fifteenth-century Italian painting contains a UFO (*right*: a close-up view).

Other Planets

If there are UFOs, where are they from? Scientists have detected numerous "extrasolar planets" beyond our Solar System. But can they support life?

Evidence for the existence of actual extrasolar planets was first reported in the mid-1990s. By 2004, well over one hundred had been found. The methods used by astronomers could detect only very large planets quite unlike Earth. But there were indications that planet systems like ours might exist. In the mid-1990s, for example, astronomers observed disks surrounding young stars located in the Orion Nebula, a giant cloud of gas and dust in the constellation Orion. These disks, called proplyds, seemed to be like the one our Sun's planets came from. Oxygen and carbon — substances crucial for life as we know it — were first detected in the atmosphere of an extrasolar planet in 2004. The planet, however, seemed unlikely to be capable of supporting life.

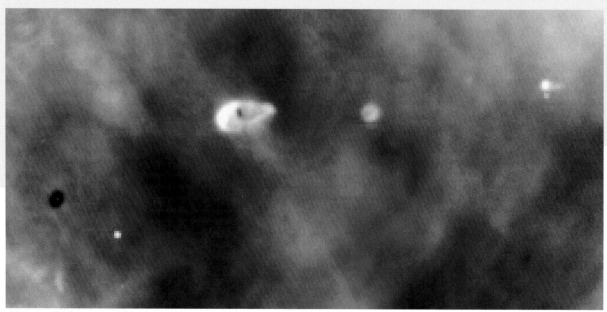

Above: A close-up of some of the proplyds, or protoplanetary disks of gas and dust, from the photo at *right*. The area shown is only about 0.14 light-year across.

The Orion Nebula, which lies some 1,500 light-years from Earth, is known as a region where stars are being born. This view of the nebula, taken by the Hubble Space Telescope in 1993, shows a number of young stars with gas and dust in orbit around them. The gas and dust are in the form of proplyds, or protoplanetary disks, that might become planets.

Otherworldly

Is it possible there may be life on other worlds? Yes! After all, there may be as many as 400 billion stars in our Galaxy, and there are more than 100 billion other galaxies. Among all these stars, a great many must be like the Sun and have planets like Earth.

J. Allen Hynek investigated 10,000 UFO sightings and concluded that about 500 could not be explained satisfactorily. By the time he died in 1986, however, he still had not been able to turn up any scientific evidence that would prove the existence of alien spaceships.

While most scientists are skeptical about UFOs, many believe alien life is possible — even likely. Large radio telescopes and other instruments are used by scientists to look for signals that could be signs of intelligent life on other worlds. Although no signals have yet been detected, some scientists believe that careful searches will eventually find evidence of other civilizations in the distant reaches of the Universe.

Left: An artist's conception of a family from another world enjoying an outing. Of the billions upon billions of stars in the Universe, couldn't at least a few million support planets with intelligent life?

Fact File: Distant and Close Encounters

People report encountering UFOs in many ways. J. Allen Hynek studied these ways and came up with two basic types of UFO encounters – distant sightings and close encounters.

In a distant sighting, a UFO appears too far away for anyone to determine what it might be or to describe it in detail. On the other hand, when people report a UFO at close range, it is called a close encounter. There are three kinds of close encounters, as defined by Hynek. These are referred to as close encounters of the first kind, second kind, and third kind.

1. Close Encounters of the First Kind – Sighting UFOs at Close Range

Most people who encounter UFOs only see them. In this kind of encounter, the UFO does not leave any physical evidence. Many people describe the UFO in detail, but even this kind of close encounter is rare.

Right: In this illustration of a close encounter of the first kind, a UFO hovers over a ship at sea. It is close enough to be sighted, reported, and even photographed by people on board the ship. But it has left no physical evidence. Many people doubt even photographic evidence of this kind of encounter.

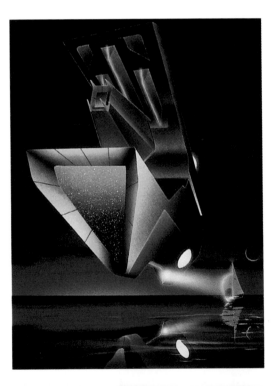

2. Close Encounters of the Second Kind – Physical Evidence or Effects from UFOs

Some people report that a UFO they have encountered leaves some kind of physical evidence, such as marks on the ground. Or they sometimes say that the presence of a UFO made them feel sick or that the UFO caused strange smells or sensations such as static electricity, strong magnetism, and heat.

Right: In this photograph of a possible close encounter of the second kind, authorities examine a presumed UFO landing site near Richmond, Virginia, in 1967. Most evidence of this sort is eventually found not to be from a flying saucer.

3. Close Encounters of the Third Kind – Sighting or Contacting Beings in or around UFOs

When people report seeing, contacting, or feeling the presence of beings in or near a UFO, Hynek determined they are reporting a close encounter of the third kind.

Above: This painting of a close encounter of the third kind illustrates one man's statement of having been taken by a saucerlike craft to a giant "mother ship" high above Earth. There, he claimed, he met with handsome humanoids from the planet Venus.

What Should You Do if You Encounter a UFO?

• Don't panic.

• Remember what *UFO* means – unidentified flying object. *Unidentified* only means that you don't know what it is. Most objects people think of as UFOs really can be identified and explained.

• People often see bright stars, planets, comets, meteors, satellites, airplanes, and even birds – but think they see something else. Sometimes, unusual weather conditions make ordinary objects in the sky look unusual. So remember that a UFO is probably nothing to be frightened of. It's just something that you cannot identify – at least when you first see it.

• If you can, ask someone else – a parent, teacher, or other adult – to look at the UFO with you. Chances are they can tell you what it really is.

• Sometimes, newspapers and television and radio news programs can tell you what a UFO really was. When a satellite falls to Earth or when a meteor shower happens, it is news!

• If you have tried to find out about a UFO and still don't know what it is, ask an adult for more help. Sometimes, people at a museum or planetarium might be able to explain what a UFO you have seen really is.

29

More Books about UFOs

Encyclopedia of Extraterrestrial Encounters. Ronald D. Story, editor (New American Library)
Space Aliens. Steve Parker (Raintree Steck-Vaughn)
The UFO Magazine UFO Encyclopedia. William Birnes (Pocket Books)
UFOs. Jacqueline Laks Gorman (Gareth Stevens)
UFOs. Terry O'Neill, editor (Greenhaven Press)
What Really Happened in Roswell? Kathleen Krull (HarperCollins)

DVDs

UFO Pilot Sightings. (Multimedia 2000)
UFOs & Aliens. (Questar)
Ultimate UFO: The Complete Evidence. (Central Park Media)

Web Sites

The Internet sites listed here can help you learn more about UFOs, extrasolar planets, and the possibility of life in the Universe beyond Earth.

Extrasolar Visions. www.extrasolar.net/
J. Allen Hynek Center for UFO Studies. www.cufos.org/
National UFO Reporting Center. www.ufocenter.com/
PlanetQuest: The Search for Another Earth. planetquest.jpl.nasa.gov/
SETI Institute. www.seti-inst.edu/
Space.com: Search for Extraterrestrial Life and SETI. www.space.com/searchforlife/

Places to Visit

Here are some museums and centers where you can find exhibits on astronomy and on worlds beyond our Earth.

Adler Planetarium and Astronomy Museum
1300 S. Lake Shore Drive
Chicago, Illinois 60605

American Museum of Natural History
Rose Center for Earth and Space
Central Park West at 79th Street
New York, NY 10024

International UFO Museum and Research Center
114 North Main Street
Roswell, New Mexico 88203

National Air and Space Museum
Smithsonian Institution
6th and Independence Avenue SW
Washington, DC 20560

Odyssium
11211 142nd Street
Edmonton, Alberta T5M4A1
Canada

StarDome Observatory
One Tree Hill Domain, off Manukau Road
Royal Oak, Auckland
New Zealand

Glossary

alien: in this book, a being from some place other than Earth.

atmosphere: the gases that surround a planet, star, or moon.

ball lightning: an unusual form of lightning that is shaped like a ball.

close encounters of the first kind: UFO sightings at close range, according to a system developed by astronomer J. Allen Hynek. In this kind of sighting, other than the stories people tell of having seen them nearby, no actual physical evidence of an encounter with UFOs exists.

close encounters of the second kind: encounters with UFOs after which there remains some kind of physical evidence or effects.

close encounters of the third kind: encounters with UFOs in which people report seeing, physically contacting, or feeling the presence of living beings in or near a UFO.

comet: a small object in space made of ice, rock, and dust. When its orbit brings it closer to the Sun, it develops a tail of gas and dust.

developer: in this book, a chemical used to bring out the image on exposed photographic film. Developer can also be used to change an image to create misleading results.

extrasolar planets: planets beyond our Solar System. Such planets orbit a star other than our Sun.

galaxy: a large grouping of stars, gas, and dust that exists in the Universe. Our Galaxy is known as the Milky Way.

hoax: an act that is intended to deceive.

Hubble Space Telescope: an artificial satellite containing a telescope and related instruments that was placed in orbit around Earth in 1990.

humanoid: a being that looks like a human or has human features.

light-year: the distance traveled by light in one year - nearly 6 trillion miles (9.5 trillion kilometers).

meteor: a meteoroid, or lump of rock or metal, that has entered Earth's atmosphere from space. Also, the bright streak of light made as the meteoroid enters or moves through the atmosphere.

nebula: a large cloud of gas and dust in space.

negative: in this book, a piece of photographic film that is used to produce a photograph.

orbit: the path that one celestial object follows as it circles around another.

phenomena: remarkable occurrences or facts in the Universe.

proplyd: a "protoplanetary disk," that is, a disk of dust and gas that encircles a star and may eventually develop into planets.

pyramids: huge structures built by the ancient Egyptians thousands of years ago. The biggest, called the Great Pyramid, consists of some 2,300,000 blocks of stone.

skeptical: having doubts about statements that others generally feel are true.

static electricity: electricity involving electric charges that stay in one place. It appears, for example, when certain materials are rubbed together.

UFO: an abbreviation for unidentified flying object.

Universe: everything that we know exists and that we believe may exist.

Index

Born in 1920, Isaac Asimov came to the United States as a young boy from his native Russia. As a young man, he was a student of biochemistry. In time, he became one of the most productive writers the world has ever known. His books cover a spectrum of topics, including science, history, language theory, fantasy, and science fiction. His brilliant imagination gained him the respect and admiration of adults and children alike. Sadly, Isaac Asimov died shortly after the publication of the first edition of *Isaac Asimov's Library of the Universe.*

The publishers wish to thank the following for permission to reproduce copyright material: front cover, 3, 10, 16 (lower), 18 (both), 20 (right), 28 (lower), © Fortean Picture Library; 4, © Tsutomu Nakayama/Fortean Picture Library; 5, 6, 8, 21, 29, © David A. Hardy; 7, 17, Courtesy of Julian Baum; 9 (both), © Gary Milburn/Tom Stack and Associates; 11, 14 (left), 16 (upper), © Julian Baum 1988; 12-13 © Janet & Colin Bord/Fortean Picture Library; 14 (right), National Severe Storms Laboratory; 15 (upper), NASA; 15 (lower), © Buff Corsi/Tom Stack and Associates; 19, © Peregrine Mendoza/Fortean Picture Library; 20 (left), © Dennis Stacy/Fortean Picture Library; 22, 23, J. Allen Hynek Center for UFO Studies; 24, 25, C. R. O'Dell/Rice University/NASA; 26-27, © MariLynn Flynn 1988; 28 (upper), © Mark Dowman.

T 8260

DATE DUE